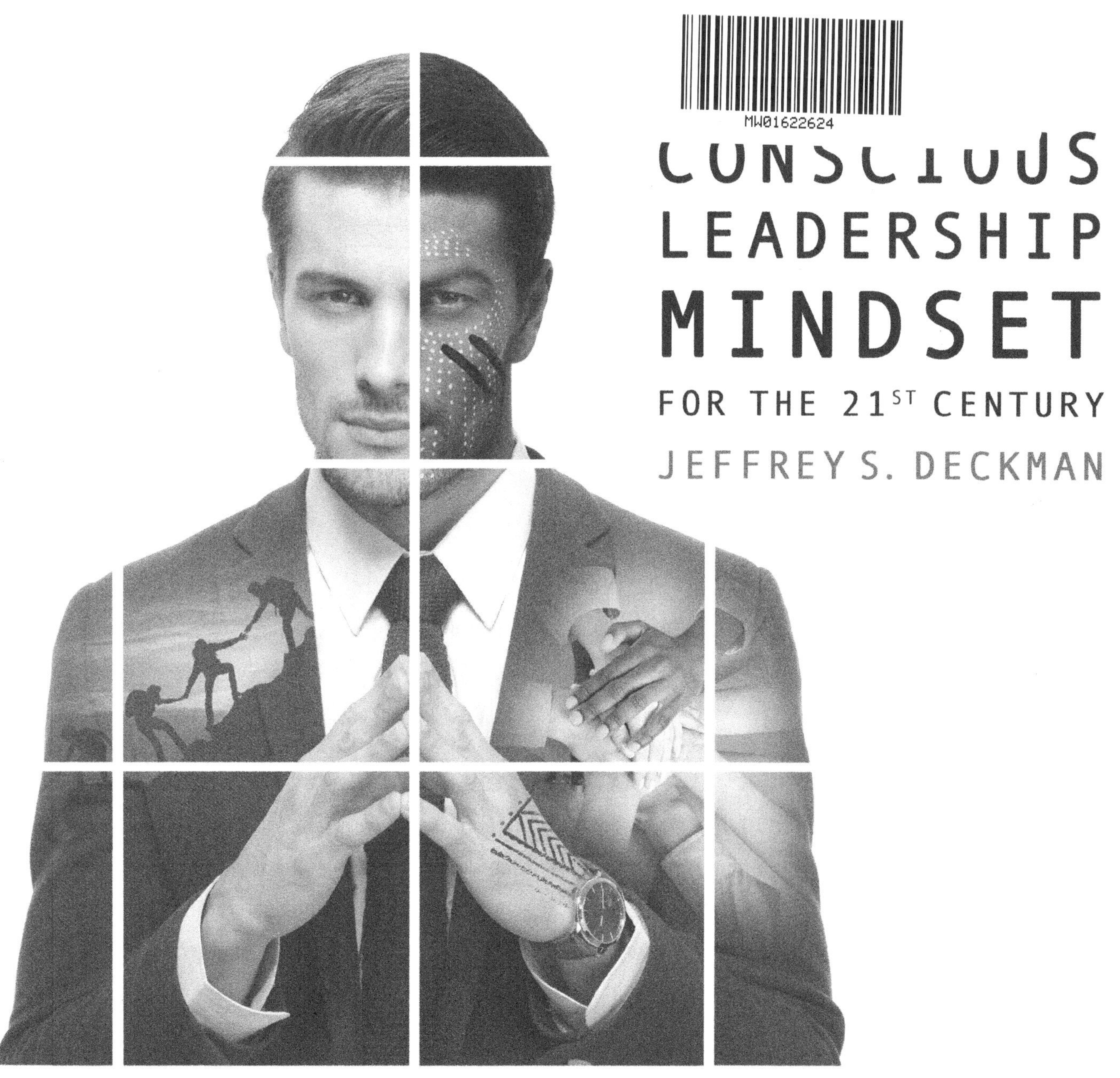

CONSCIOUS LEADERSHIP MINDSET FOR THE 21ST CENTURY

JEFFREY S. DECKMAN

INSIGHT FOR LEADING CHANGE, IMPROVING EMPLOYEE ENGAGEMENT, *AND* ACHIEVING EXTRAORDINARY RESULTS

DEVELOPING THE CONSCIOUS LEADERSHIP MINDSET FOR THE 21ST CENTURY

Insight for Leading Change, Improving Employee Engagement, and Achieving Extraordinary Results

Conscious Leadership Series

JEFFREY S. DECKMAN

ISBN: 978-1-7337266-0-3

Published by: Capability Accelerators, Inc.

Quantity Discounts Available

Quantity discounts for DEVELOPING THE CONSCIOUS LEADERSHIP MINDSET FOR THE 21ST CENTURY are available for groups, companies, and organizations, and schools.

For a discount schedule please contact: Merchandise@JefferyDeckman.com

PRAISE

The beauty of the Conscious Leadership Book Series is that it engages you in the way you learn and in doing so feels like a very well-tailored solution to your becoming the leader you want to be. It feels as if Jeffrey Deckman is talking with you instead of at or over you and that makes it easy to learn in a very comfortable way.

MARK GOULSTON, author, *Just Listen, Discover the Secret to Getting Through to Absolutely Anyone*

Developing the Conscious Leader Mindset for the 21st Century is a wisdom sharing book that will instantly resonate with you. The integrated approach shows how you can develop as a leader, the best ways to engage employees, and how to develop a culture that supports conscious leadership. By far, this is the best leadership book I've ever read!

JACK BEAUREGARD, author and CEO Successful Transition Planning Institute

The Conscious Leadership Book Series gets to the heart of the matter in leadership. The formula is always valid—higher levels of consciousness of leadership consistently generate a healthier, high-performance culture, increased employee engagement, and higher levels of customer satisfaction. Jeffrey has hit the nail on the head with this book!

DR. MARC B. COOPER, President of Insight Coaching and Consulting. Author of *Source, The Twelve Laws of Leadership and The Elder*

> *Jeffrey Deckman has provided a practical and insightful guide for leaders interested in elevating employee engagement, attracting and retaining talented employees, and aligning an organization behind a compelling vision. He brings a fresh perspective about leadership, while grounding his writing in a deep understanding of how and why leaders succeed and fail.*
>
> **MICHAEL ROBERTO,** Author of *Unlocking Creativity, Trustee Professor of Management* – Bryant University

> *What stands out most about this book is that the concepts presented are simple yet powerful. Jeffrey shows you who great leaders need to be in this Age of Innovation and has distilled his concepts into digestible tactics you can put into immediate action. He will challenge you and inspire you to think beyond what you thought was possible. This is one resource you will want by your side as you navigate your journey as a leader.*
>
> **JEAN MARIE DIGIOVANNA**, Leadership Speaker, Executive Coach, and Founder of Workshop University

> *I experienced Jeffrey Deckman's work first hand when I was a political candidate and now as House Minority Leader in the Rhode Island State House. If every elected official read this book and committed to becoming a more conscious leader, the people would be much better served by their government. In this book, Deckman flips the script for a new generation of leadership and in doing so empowers any type of twenty-first century organization to achieve their potential.*
>
> **BLAKE FILIPPI**, Minority Leader, Rhode Island House of Representatives

“ *All roads have led Jeffrey Deckman to write this book. He shares what he's learned from his decades-long leadership journey through this easy-to-use, thought provoking curriculum. It gives leaders at all levels the opportunity to reflect on their own leadership style, and how a shift in mindset will not only make your role more enjoyable and your employees more engaged but will also increase your organization's bottom line. Take your first steps with Jeffrey on your journey to conscious leadership. You won't regret it.*

JO-ANN SCHOFIELD, CEO MENTOR Rhode Island

“ *Jeff's strength has always been his distinctive ability to penetrate the surface and come at issues with unique insights that turn the traditional on its axis. He's never been willing to accept the status quo, especially when it is clear it is not working. His approach to conscious leadership provides the tools for anyone at any level of experience to grasp the concept being presented and then to put it into practice in the real world. If you want to fast track your transformation into a twenty-first century conscious leader then this book is definitely a must-read.*

PATRICIA MORGAN, Rhode Island state Representative, former House Minority Leader and Gubernatorial Candidate, 2018

“ *I had the opportunity to take part in a course taught by Jeff Deckman several years ago that contained the framework for the tenets of this book. In a day and age that is increasingly focused on the bottom line, his principles of the conscious leader are more important than ever. Deckman empowers individuals with the tools they need to not only be successful leaders of transfor-*

mative organizations at any level, but also enables them to possess a greater personal knowledge of themselves and others that is invaluable in any setting in which they are looking to impact positive change.

KATE NAGLE, News Editor, GoLocalProv.com

“ *Developing the Conscious Leadership Mindset is a compelling read that not only inspires but serves as a self-development guide for becoming an effective and modern leader. It thoughtfully plots a customizable pathway for personal and professional development. Written in straightforward prose, Deckman's book lives and breathes the dynamic energy that will breed the kind of awareness truly successful leaders must embrace. Leaders willing to follow this consciousness-raising journey will change the world. I know because Deckman was once my mentor and*

whenever I struggle in a leadership role, I think, 'How would Jeff deal with this?

KATHERINE O'DEA, Co-Founder Circular Economy Strategists

“ *Developing the Conscious Leadership Mindset offers the framework and tools to lead effectively in the modern workplace. Rather than preach to readers about what they are doing wrong, he offers evidenced-based methods that more deeply engage and connect with employees. Think of it as an experiential workshop in book form. Jeffrey's tools empower readers to develop their personal leadership styles to address their organizational challenges.*

LISA TENER, Book Development Coach

I remember vividly the first time I met Jeff Deckman—he was speaking from the perspective of an industry partner in a workforce development initiative. I said to myself that here is stand-up guy, someone who really gets what it means to be a leader in these complex times. Impressed by his presentation, I went up to him after his talk to ask if he would chair the Rhode Island Technology Council. He accepted and did a fantastic job in that role, while all the while growing his own companies. I have partnered with him on many successful projects since then, and what I can tell you is that the Jeff you read on these pages is the Jeff I have seen in action as a leader. He's the real deal.

KIP BERGSTROM, Principal Rebooting New England, former Deputy Commissioner, Connecticut Dept. of Economic and Community Dev.

DEDICATION

To my dad, Paul DuPont Deckman, Sr.

The only thing greater than your cool name is the love you have shown me, the lessons you have taught me, and the example you have been for me.

My dad. My mentor. My hero. Thanks for all of it, Pop.

To my future grandson, Anthony Tullio Harris, Jr., who will be born the same month and the same year this book is being published. I already know you and I already love you.

Welcome to our tribe.

ACKNOWLEDGEMENTS

This book would never have been written without the help of many people who have given of their time, their energy, their advice, and their encouragement.

First and foremost, thank you, Donna Rustigian Mac. This work would not exist in this form without your listening, your contributions, and your constant reminder that it needed to be shared.

You always believed in me and the importance of this work. Thank you for everything forever.

To my three adult children, Allison, Justin, and Tyler. I truly admire each of you. You inspire me to contribute positively to your world. So I try to.

To John Clarke, Kip Bergstrom, Robert Leaver, and Larry Quick. Each of you have had a profound impact on my ability to see beyond the horizon and to manifest what is possible.

To Michelle Girasole and Bob Salvas. There were times when the only reason I took the next step on this path was because you both were there along side of me.

To Dave Englund and Sal Sauco of Englund Studios. Your coining of the phrase "Jeffisms" as you were developing my website led to the idea to make this the first book in the series.

To Steve Beauvais, Joyce Strause, and Bill Annino, Jr. Each of you inspired and challenged me to look beyond my blind spots and to grow beyond my ego to become a far more conscious leader than I ever could have without you.

To my publisher Howard VanEs of Let's Write Books, Inc. You helped me to both see that this book could be published, and that you were the best one to do it. Everything clicked once we clicked.

To my publicist, Melissa Sones. You are a brilliant force of nature. Because of you this work will help many more people than I ever could have imagined.

To Lisa Tener. You are clearly the best book writing coach and book proposal editor in the country. Your guidance has been instrumental and invaluable.

To Dr. Jody Noe, MS. ND. After you guided me mentally, physically, and spiritually through my bout with cancer, you then helped me to remember what I came here to do in this life. This book is part of that.

And finally, to Sri Harold Klemp for the tools and teachings you have provided that have helped me expand my consciousness, my ability to love myself and others more, and for exposing me to the joys of being of service.

CONTENTS

INTRODUCTION

"In times of great change learners inherit the earth; while the learned find themselves beautifully equipped to deal with a world that no longer exists."

—Eric Hoffer, "The American Philosopher"

We are facing a severe leadership crisis in both the front office and on the front lines of business. This is evidenced by the fact that, year after year, Gallup's State of American Workplace Report states that the average employee engagement figures never rise much above 30 percent at a cost of over $500-billion-dollars in lost productivity annually.[1]

In comparison, world class companies enjoy 70 percent employee engagement figures and significantly higher profits as a result.

While these percentages and losses are clearly unacceptable, they have been this low for so long that they have become accepted by many well-meaning management teams. And while they may be the norm, they are increasingly becoming far too expensive for companies in the modern knowledge economy—in which almost all profitability is driven by employee engagement.

1 This report presents an unparalleled look into the modern workforce. It is based on Gallup's in-depth research and study data from over 195,000 employees and over 31 million respondents. The report provides invaluable information on the current conditions of the modern workplace and suggestions on how to increase employee engagement in the post-industrial age knowledge economy. To download a copy Google "Gallup 2017 State of American Workplace."

Further Gallup research reveals that managers account for at least 70 percent of the variance in employee engagement scores. In other words, poor leadership skills are the reasons behind poor engagement levels.

Now, before we send the posse out to round up all the bad managers and run them out of town, we need to take a moment to ask ourselves: "Why are there so many 'bad' managers out there?"

Clearly, there aren't that many people who have exceled enough, for long enough, who all of a sudden have become bad people! That defies both logic and human nature. Logic dictates there is something else at work causing excellent employees to become bad managers.

It's the Models Not the Managers

So, if bad people aren't the cause for so much bad leadership, what is?

My experiences have led me to believe the problem is occurring because the level of sophistication and consciousness of the modern worker has outgrown the limiting, paternalistic, and even patronizing leadership models and methods that have defined the Industrial Age for over two centuries.

The Industrial Age command and control, top-down, authoritative, and hierarchical leadership models and methods that were necessary to successfully build the largest armies, fight the largest wars, and then to build the largest mega-corporations the world has ever seen during the twentieth century's Industrial Age have become too limiting, too controlling, and too wasteful of vital human capital to be effective in the modern Innovation Age and knowledge economy it has birthed.

The new millennium has brought with it an explosion and proliferation of both technology and individualism—each of which are exponentially evolving at break-neck speeds. The result is rapidly increasing levels of organizational complexity and individual independence that is rendering the traditional leadership models so ineffective that they are quickly becoming liabilities.

We currently have five of the most independent minded, educated, and mobile generations in the history of humanity in the workforce. These people not only expect to be respected and empowered; they demand it. They are also demanding they be approached differently by management. And if they aren't, their response is to either move slower or to move on. Both of which impacts performance and profits.

As leaders, it is imperative that we not only accept this reality but that we begin actively exploring, experimenting with, and embracing new leadership mindsets, models, and methods that free, engage, and empower the human capital in ways that increases morale, engagement, and profits while decreasing stress and conflict.

But we also must be careful not to get caught up in sexy fads that are based upon theories instead of realities.

About the Conscious Leadership Series

After having spent thirty years boot strapping and building two of my own multi-million-dollar companies, I have spent the last decade as a leadership and organizational consultant, and a partner in a think tank, developing and field-testing next generation leadership and organizational models that are helping other folks to build theirs.

The result of which is the Conscious Leadership book series.

This first book in the series focuses upon helping you to understand, practice, and begin mastering a new leadership mindset designed for today's sophisticated workforce.

The second book outlines a new organizational model that reveals three powerful, yet almost invisible, dynamics that drive all performance and profits in organizations. Those drivers are tribes, knowledge networks, and cultures. While constantly present and very powerful, they remain hidden from view when looking at your organization through the lens of the org chart. I refer to the combination of these three forces as the organization trinity.

The third book in the series provides a highly effective eight-step conscious leadership methodology designed to give you the tools needed to identify, mobilize, and leverage more of the collective genius and energies of today's multi-generational, multi-gendered, and multi-ethnic workforce.

The system is called the Bigger Know Principles of Leadership and is based upon the premise that: "You know what you know. They know what they know. And together, you have a Bigger Know." Its focus is to help the leader to use communication, collaboration, and facilitation to increase employee engagement.

Individually, each book will introduce and thoroughly explain the new concepts each is focused upon. Collectively, they provide you with the mindsets, models, and methods required for you to begin learning the new twenty-first century leadership skills necessary to better build a twenty-first century-ready organization and to better engage the twenty-first century worker.

My hope is that you can use the information, insights, and knowledge I have gained over the past forty years on the front lines of management to shorten your learning curves as you seek to increase your impact and effectiveness as a leader of the modern workforce.

If my work helps you accomplish your goals, then I will have accomplished mine.

TWO FREE BONUSES

Bonus #1: Measure the Impact of Employee Engagement on Profitability

The impact of employee engagement (EE) has a direct impact on profitability, but the question has always been how and how much. This paper reveals a financial formula (EE=EBITDA) that explains the relationship between the two. It then shows how an organization with a $2-million-dollar payroll that increases its employee engagement by only 5 percent can increase profitability by $50,000.00 per year.

Bonus #2: Win Challenging Conversations with the Three Most Challenging Types of Employees

The most difficult employee for the conscientious manager is the unconscientious employee. Each time you try to get them to address their issues, you meet up with one of three versions of this employee: the arguer, the denier, or the avoider.

This white paper provides a fool proof method of getting to the bottom of their issue, get your point across, and control the direction of the conversation with even the slipperiest of personalities.

Download both bonuses at www.JeffreyDeckman.com/bonuses

HOW TO USE THIS BOOK

While you are certainly free to use this book in whatever way you find most enjoyable and effective, below are some suggestions on how you can use it as highly effective leadership development tool for yourself and those in your organization.

The goal of this book is to simultaneously serve as a thought provoker, a teaching tool, and an operational field manual that can be used as the basis for a self-teaching curriculum you, and your entire team, can use to begin the challenging work of transforming your leadership skills to meet the challenges of the modern workforce, which is, without question, the most demanding and independent minded workforce in the history of business.

It is designed to be a practical resource you can refer to as needed when you are facing an impending challenge or when you want to learn more about a specific aspect of conscious leadership.

To get the best long-term results, I suggest you and your team take time to work through this body of work and allow for discussion, contemplation, and realizations. Let it seep in and work for you.

The shifting of consciousness and belief systems takes time and patience. We can no more rush the unfolding of either than we can rush the unfolding of a flower's petals. Each takes time and must follow the laws of nature.

So, trust the process and trust *your* process. Then trust that you will get exactly what you need when you are ready for it.

But most of all, enjoy your journey.

The Design

This book features fifty-two tools, insights, realizations, and suggestions separated into three chapters, representing three phases along the path of conscious leadership.

Each chapter is further broken down into subcategories focused upon addressing specific challenges or explaining dynamics that are relevant to that chapter and which are important to your development as a more conscious leader.

The selections in this book are designed to be read slowly, consumed, contemplated about, pondered over, journaled about, and even argued with. But mostly, they are to be considered with an open mind, experimented with, and applied under real world conditions.

It is through their application that the learning occurs, and the benefits realized. Along the way, your experiences, your questions, and confusing moments will be the catalysts for the "a-ha" moments that will lead you to new levels of leadership consciousness and understanding.

As you travel through your journey, try to do so with curiosity, optimism, and a sense of adventure. Resist the urge to make any of this work.

Refuse the tendency to turn this into another in a long list of "gotta dos" that you must discipline your way through. Instead, explore what is written and walk through this body of work with your heart open and your mind relaxed.

In doing so, you will convert a "gotta do" into a "get to do," and that will make all the difference in how you approach, absorb, and apply what is offered within these pages.

Have fun, enjoy yourself, and don't stress over any of it. You will get everything you need when you need it, and you can always refer back to any part of it to get more.

The Learning Methods

Everyone learns and absorbs information differently.

Some people like to absorb information in a stepped, structured manner which takes them through a learning arc from a beginning, through a middle, and eventually to an end that leads to a new place of understanding. Others prefer a less structured, more instinctive, approach.

Regardless, the impact of this work can only be realized when you experiment with, and apply, what is being proposed. Only by putting into practice what is written will learning and growth occur and optimum results be achieved.

Below are some suggestions for how you can make this book work best for you:

1. The Curriculum Method

Fifty-two or twenty-six-week course:

For those who want a structured curriculum, you can either review one lesson per week or two, which will make it either a fifty-two week or a twenty-six week course.

STEP 1: Scheduling: Decide upon the time frame you want to use. Select a day of the week and a time that you, and your team, will take each class. Treat it with the same discipline you would any other important career development training course. Your level of transformation is directly tied to your level of discipline.

STEP 2: Creating the learning environment and settling the mind: Find or create a quiet space. Center yourself. Try sitting with your eyes closed. Take a few moments to take a few breaths. Settle your mind. Begin relaxing and shifting your consciousness by focusing upon your breaths and your body.

STEP 3: Read the passage. Take a moment to think about what it means to you. Don't rush through this.

If you are doing this with a group, do this in silence without sharing your thoughts. Then once everyone has finished, open it up for discussion for anyone who wants to speak. Be mindful to allow each one to express their views and impressions without them being challenged. Hearing different perspectives can be both enlightening and productive. WARNING: Avoid allowing a right vs. wrong dynamic from occurring. It will shut down the process.

Then, on the top of the left-hand page under "Initial Impressions," describe your thoughts, feelings, and understanding of what the statement means to you.

Under that, next to the section titled, "How does this show up for me?" indicate what you notice about how the issue may be currently showing up in your life or organization.

STEP 4: Carry the contemplation seed with you over the next few days. See what comes to you. Let it percolate. Practice it, challenge it, and discuss it with other members of your team. Resist the urge to convince anyone of anything. Just communicate what is coming to you without being overly pushy or cerebral. Feel free to journal your thoughts along the way.

STEP 5: Note your progress. At the beginning of your next scheduled class, note any learnings, lessons, deeper understandings, and realizations that came to you during your process under the section titled, "Upon further reflection."

If you are doing this with a group, encourage conversation and sharing. Keep it conversational, non-judgmental, and safe.

STEP 6: In the section titled, "Next steps:" write to down any next steps that you would like to implement both individually and, if appropriate, as a group. If you are doing this in a group, be very careful to have the group support one another's individuality. Resist the urge to insist on group thinking. This is first and foremost and individual journey.

Note: You may decide to create a companion journal that will allow you to capture more of what you are learning than a single half page in the book will allow.

Move on to the next lesson.

2. The "Random" Method.

STEP 1: Decide whether you prefer the fifty-two-week or twenty-six-week pace.

STEP 2: Repeat steps 1 and 2 from above.

STEP 3: Once settled, "ask" to be led to the passage that will benefit you the most. With your eyes closed, open the book to a page and read it, trusting that it is what is in your best interest to explore at this time.

STEP 4: Follow steps 3 through 6.

3. The Ala-Carte Method

STEP 1: Decide whether you prefer the fifty-two-week or twenty-six-week pace.

STEP 2: Choose the specific topic you want to learn about.

STEP 3: Follow steps 1 through 6 from the Curriculum method.

4. The Book as a Field Manual

Often times over the course of your studies, real world situations will arise that need immediate attention and action. When this happens, you and your team can simply refer to the relevant sections and see which insights will assist you to address the challenge at hand.

This should be done while maintaining your regular method of study. In this way, the book will be helping you to not only develop your conscious leadership skills in a stepped manner, but it will also serve your immediate needs as they arise.

The combination of the two processes will maximize its impact.

Conclusion

In my experience of walking my path of consciousness over the past thirty years, I have learned that few realizations come quickly. Most involve many steps, some of them seemingly slow and arduous. They will appear to be yielding little progress until a tipping point is reached and a new realization or a new consciousness is achieved.

I liken this process to that of a child playing in a playground who decides to step on to the low end of a seesaw for the purpose of walking to the other end and bringing it to the ground. Initial steps are taken, effort is made, and movement is taking place, but it appears that no progress is being made towards the goal because the high end of the seesaw hasn't budged.

Then at some point, with just one more step and without warning, we hit the tipping point and immediately everything changes. What was once seemingly an all uphill struggle, yielding no results, now becomes a downhill ride. Our steps become easier, our pace quickens, our excitement returns, and we see in retrospect how all the steps were of use.

Such is the process of spiritual growth and consciousness elevation. Take your time. Trust your process. Have patience. And most importantly: Enjoy your ride.

And remember: There is never a lack of consciousness—only room for more.

CHAPTER ONE

THE FUNDAMENTALS

ESTABLISHING THE FRAMEWORK AND MINDSET

Every process begins with a framework.

Every action begins with a mindset.

"Always see the human in the human."

—Jeffrey Deckman

INITIAL IMPRESSIONS

HOW DOES THIS SHOW UP FOR ME?

UPON FURTHER REFLECTION

NEXT STEPS

LEADERSHIP IS A STATE OF CONSCIOUSNESS.

Leadership is no longer about telling people what to do. It is about understanding how to support them in doing what needs to be done.

Leadership is no longer about command and control, top-down models, and methods. It is about communication, collaboration, and facilitation.

Leadership is no longer about talking and telling. It is about connecting and listening.

Leadership is no longer about managing by org charts. It is about engaging and empowering tribes.

Leadership simply can no longer be dominated by paternalistic masculine energies. It must be equally balanced with maternalistic feminine energies.

Power without nurturing breeds weakness.

"We aren't in Kansas anymore, Toto."

1.

INITIAL IMPRESSIONS

HOW DOES THIS SHOW UP FOR ME?

UPON FURTHER REFLECTION

NEXT STEPS

THE FIRST STEP ON THE PATH TO CONSCIOUS LEADERSHIP IS AN INWARD ONE.

And so are all the rest.

To grow our consciousness, we must grow spiritually. There is no way to separate the two. Spirituality is the helium that expands and elevates our consciousness.

The spiritual path, or method, one chooses is their choice. To each their own. There are many paths, and if traveled with an open heart, curiosity, and an honest desire—they all lead to growth.

To grow our consciousness, we must want to simply because we want to. Don't make it another task on a long list of other "gotta dos" or it will drain you instead of replenish and refresh you.

Be careful not to let the head take over or the heart will be pushed out and no real growth will occur. Besides, we can't think our way to a higher consciousness.

Instead look for teachings, teachers, or create experiences that resonate with you. Look for something that you're drawn to.

It may take a while. It may happen with just one teaching or teacher, or a combination of several different ones. For instance, it could be western, eastern, Native American, or anything else. It could also be time in the woods, at the ocean, or literally anything else that opens your heart and settles your mind. Experiment and enjoy the journey.

2.

There is no way to do this wrong.

INITIAL IMPRESSIONS

HOW DOES THIS SHOW UP FOR ME?

UPON FURTHER REFLECTION

NEXT STEPS

CONSCIOUS LEADERSHIP IS NOT ABOUT WHAT YOU DO OR SAY. IT'S ABOUT BEING AWARE OF WHY AND HOW YOU DO WHAT YOU DO AND SAY.

It is about exploring and becoming conscious of the true motives and intentions behind your actions. It is about being conscious of how they affect ourselves and others.

It is about wanting to serve instead of wanting to lead. It is about using your leadership to serve others, not yourself.

At its core, it is about doing all you can to consistently act with and engage others with authenticity, integrity, and respect. (A.I.R.)

Conscious leadership is about "Leading with A.I.R."

3.

INITIAL IMPRESSIONS

HOW DOES THIS SHOW UP FOR ME?

UPON FURTHER REFLECTION

NEXT STEPS

IN THE CONTEXT OF THIS BOOK, AUTHENTICITY, INTEGRITY, AND RESPECT MEAN THE FOLLOWING:

Authenticity is about accepting who you are. It is doing your best to know yourself and having the courage and grace to accept yourself. It is about recognizing both your strengths and weaknesses without being afraid to acknowledge either.

Authenticity is about being honest with yourself and accepting yourself, and then having the courage to live your unique life in your unique way.

Integrity is about being honest with others both about who you are and how you act. It is about having and living within moral principles regardless of whether you are in public or alone.

Integrity is about valuing and living your principles regardless of their difficulty or popularity. It is about honoring your true self more than your ego. It is about who you are to yourself and with others.

Respect is about honoring both yourself and something greater than yourself. It is about respecting those who came before you, those who are in front of you, and those who must follow you.

It is about acknowledging a timeline that not only considers the present, but also the past and the future. It is about considering how your actions will impact you, those around you, and the organizations that depend upon you.

It is about being a good steward.

INITIAL IMPRESSIONS

HOW DOES THIS SHOW UP FOR ME?

UPON FURTHER REFLECTION

NEXT STEPS

“LEADING WITH A.I.R.” DOES NOT MEAN YOU WON’T HAVE BAD MOMENTS OR BAD DAYS WHERE YOU ARE COMPLETELY OFF. LEADING WITH A.I.R. IS AN OBJECTIVE TO STRIVE FOR.

It is a North Star that helps guide you back on track when you go astray.

When you do slip, which you will, you can quickly use A.I.R. to get back on track by:

1. Being authentic and acknowledging the error.
2. Having integrity by accepting responsibility and doing the next right thing.
3. Showing respect to yourself and others by re-establishing yourself on your path.
4. Learn from your mistake and continue to move forward, wiser for the experience.

5.

INITIAL IMPRESSIONS

HOW DOES THIS SHOW UP FOR ME?

UPON FURTHER REFLECTION

NEXT STEPS

THE SIMPLEST AND SUREST WAY TO ESTABLISH YOURSELF ON THE PATH OF CONSCIOUS LEADERSHIP IS TO COMMIT TO AND HOLD YOURSELF ACCOUNTABLE TO LIVE, BREATHE, AND LEAD WITH A.I.R.

...Then repeat, repeat and repeat again.

6.

INITIAL IMPRESSIONS

HOW DOES THIS SHOW UP FOR ME?

UPON FURTHER REFLECTION

NEXT STEPS

CONSCIOUS LEADERSHIP IS NOT ABOUT GETTING YOURSELF AND OTHERS TO DO MORE. IT IS ABOUT BECOMING MORE.

It is not about trying to get you and others to do things right. It is about committing yourself and others to do the right thing.

It is not about what you are doing. It is about why you are doing what you are doing and who you are while doing it.

Conscious leadership is about leading in a way that fully considers and takes benefit from everything within our sphere of influence.

7.

THE POWER OF THE "BIGGER KNOW"

There is a Bigger Know.

Everyone you will ever meet knows something you don't.

This means that everywhere you go there is a Bigger Know.

You know what you know.

They know what they know.

Together we have a Bigger Know.*

**Principle 1 of The Bigger Know Principles of Leadership*

INITIAL IMPRESSIONS

HOW DOES THIS SHOW UP FOR ME?

UPON FURTHER REFLECTION

NEXT STEPS

THE PEOPLE IN YOUR ORGANIZATION REPRESENT A LIVING, BREATHING, WALKING, AND TALKING LIBRARY THAT NEVER STOPS LEARNING OR GROWING.

They possess a collective genius and incredibly powerful energies. However, these resources are mostly unrecognized and therefore are mostly untapped.

The combination of their genius and energies is their Bigger Know.

Collectively, these people know more about what makes the organization work and not work than you or I can ever hope to know. They see every aspect of it better than us.

Collectively, they know the cause of most all of the problems we face and can predict new ones. Because of this, they are an invaluable resource in finding realistic solutions and innovative approaches to increase performance and profits.

They also want to share what they know. But they have to be asked, engaged in a dialogue, and have their input respected and fairly considered.

So, the first step in accessing their Bigger Know is to first recognize its existence. Then we must engage it, encourage it, and incentivize it so that you can monetize it for the benefit of all involved.

INITIAL IMPRESSIONS

HOW DOES THIS SHOW UP FOR ME?

UPON FURTHER REFLECTION

NEXT STEPS

THE BIGGER KNOW RESIDES WITHIN FOUR LAYERS OF THINKING. I REFER TO THESE LAYERS AS "THE FOUR I'S OF INNOVATION." THEY ARE INTELLIGENCE, IDEAS, INSIGHTS, AND INTUITION.

Intelligence is the data and information we already possess or can gather through known sources. It represents "what we know we know."

Ideas are new mental images and concepts generated from pieces of intelligence. They represent "what we create from what we know."

Insight is perceiving the inward nature of something or gaining a penetrating mental vision. Often, these insights appear out of nowhere and have a high degree of accuracy. This is often referred to as an "a-ha" moment. Insights represent what we know through flash knowing.

Intuition is instinctive knowing without a rational process or logical explanation. It seemingly appears from the ether and is often referred to as a "hunch" or a "gut feeling" and tends to nag at us if we don't explore or express it. It is "what we know we know without knowing how we know."

When seeking to address a challenge, we as leaders must create the conditions
9. for people to feel safe enough to freely flow between, and to contribute from, each of these layers as you seek to maximize and then leverage the power of the Bigger Know.

INITIAL IMPRESSIONS

HOW DOES THIS SHOW UP FOR ME?

UPON FURTHER REFLECTION

NEXT STEPS

ANYTIME TWO OR MORE PEOPLE ASSEMBLE, A BIGGER KNOW IS CREATED. IT IS IMPOSSIBLE FOR IT NOT TO BE. BUT IT IS NOT ALWAYS ACCESSIBLE BECAUSE IT OFTEN GETS BLOCKED.

What blocks it?

Egos

> *Bombastic egos that overpower others*
>
> *Bashful egos that won't share their thinking*
>
> *Brutish egos who must dominate and control*
>
> *Brilliant egos that already "know so much"*

When the ego dominates, the Bigger Know hibernates. Wisdom does not fight for attention from fools.

The less the Bigger Know is active and engaged, the more thinking and work the leader must do on their own and the more mistakes that will be made.

Practice looking for it. Be aware of when the Bigger Know is active and when it isn't, and why. As you do, you will become more conscious of the dynamics that affect it.

It is a fascinating force.

10.

INITIAL IMPRESSIONS

HOW DOES THIS SHOW UP FOR ME?

UPON FURTHER REFLECTION

NEXT STEPS

AFTER ACKNOWLEDGING THE IMPACT OF EGO ON THE BIGGER KNOW, THE FIRST STEP IN LESSENING ITS IMPACT IS TO "DOMESTICATE THE DOG."*

Egos are like dogs. If they are not properly trained, they growl, bite, jump on people, and stick their noses in inappropriate places.

And just as how one dog barking activates other dogs to start barking, one barking ego activates other egos to start barking. If left unchecked, so many dogs become activated that they dominate the environment.

In contrast, the genius of the Bigger Know is like a cat: it appears when the conditions are right, disappears when they aren't, and it doesn't respond to commands to appear.

So just as you will never find a cat around a pack of untrained dogs, the genius of the Bigger Know will never appear in a roomful of egos.

This means that one of our primary roles as a conscious leader is to "domesticate the dogs" in the room, especially our own. Otherwise your company will be run by dogs.

Begin observing how this dynamic occurs in your organization. Think about times when you have seen it play out and the impact it has had.

11.

**Principle #2 of The Bigger Know Principles of Leadership.*

INITIAL IMPRESSIONS

HOW DOES THIS SHOW UP FOR ME?

UPON FURTHER REFLECTION

NEXT STEPS

ONCE YOU'VE CALMED THE DOGS, THE NEXT CHALLENGE IS TO RELEASE THE POWER OF THE BIGGER KNOW INTO YOUR ORGANIZATION. THIS PROCESS BEGINS WITH ASKING AND INVITING QUESTIONS, AND THEN TRULY LISTENING.*

Asking questions begins with being genuinely curious about knowing another's perspective and the reasons behind it. Then, once heard, the leader must assess the input on its merits without prejudices to determine what has value and what may not.

Inviting questions begins with being genuinely interested in having them participate as an equal in the conversation. It's inviting them to ask anything they need to know in order to understand, and even question, the predominant thinking.

Then when you truly listen to people, and you treat their input with respect, they will feel that respect and will participate more freely. This increases your access to their Bigger Know.

Listening is the language of respect.

Respect is the key that unlocks the door to the Bigger Know.

12.

Beware if you find yourself hesitant of having your thinking questioned. Also notice when you find yourself becoming too impatient, or unwilling to listen. These are signs that your dog is trying to take over.

**Principle #3 of The Bigger Know Principles of Leadership.*

INITIAL IMPRESSIONS

HOW DOES THIS SHOW UP FOR ME?

UPON FURTHER REFLECTION

NEXT STEPS

13.

MOST OF US ARE NOT GOOD LISTENERS. STUDIES HAVE SHOWN THAT PEOPLE ONLY LISTEN FOR SEVEN SECONDS BEFORE WANTING TO INTERRUPT.

We're almost always blind to our poor listening skills and our tendency to interrupt. Yet both significantly reduce our leadership abilities because, by interrupting or not listening, we are disrespecting those around us. This causes them to shut down which then causes us to lose access to their Bigger Know.

The next time you find yourself wanting to interrupt someone, pause and think of this acronym: W.A.I.T.

It has a dual meaning that stands for:

"Why Am I Talking?"

&

"What Am I Teaching?"

Resist the urge to make yourself, or your thinking, the most important part of every conversation. This is a natural response, but it is highly counterproductive.

Let the person finish their sentence. Let them finish their thought. Only then can you get the full picture of their viewpoint. Only then can you know how to proceed.

In doing so, you are not only practicing putting your "dog on a leash" but you are teaching others to do the same.

INITIAL IMPRESSIONS

HOW DOES THIS SHOW UP FOR ME?

UPON FURTHER REFLECTION

NEXT STEPS

NOT ALL THOUGHTS SHARED ARE RELEVANT OR VALUABLE TO AN ISSUE AT HAND. THIS IS WHERE THE LAW OF "VIVEKA" (OR WISE DISCRIMINATION) COMES INTO PLAY.

As conscious leaders, we keep our brainstorming sessions on point and on task while still allowing room for free-flowing thoughts that are necessary for creativity, ideation, and innovation. In other words, we must strike a balance that allows for people to contribute from any layer of the "four I's of innovation" as they flow from linear thought to intuitive thinking while still maintaining relevance.

This requires the leader to become an astute conductor of conversations. We must practice discerning the relevant from the irrelevant, the important from the unimportant, and allowing for thoughts to be expressed without allowing anything to bog the process down.

We also have to develop the tolerance and patience to allow for productive, discriminative inquiry while managing any unproductive emotions and egos generated by such inquiries. Especially our own.

As leaders, we must strive to achieve a delicate balance between being a participant, a facilitator, and an arbiter in the right measure, at the right time, and in the right places.

14. This will both test and build your conscious leadership skills in powerful ways. It will also make you a master at accessing and maximizing the power of your Bigger Know.

THE ORGANIZATIONAL TRINITY—TRIBES, KNOWLEDGE NETWORKS, AND CULTURES

Hidden behind the org chart are three powerful forces responsible for how nearly all work gets done in any organization. They are tribes, knowledge networks, and cultures.

Tribes are the source of the muscle that does all the work. Knowledge networks are the source of the brains that do all the thinking. And cultures are the source of the heart that holds us all together.

As such, conscious leadership is less about managing the people and more about managing the conditions that unleash the power of the *organizational trinity*.

INITIAL IMPRESSIONS

HOW DOES THIS SHOW UP FOR ME?

UPON FURTHER REFLECTION

NEXT STEPS

KEY COMPONENTS OF HEALTHY BUSINESS TRIBES:

- Meritocracy, equity, and fairness
- Leaders who serve as elders
- Members who serve as stewards
- Clear guidelines and expectations
- Open communications between the front office and the front lines
- A shared sense of accountability and a sense of responsibility
- Clearly defined and fairly enforced consequences
- A sense of belonging and inclusion
- A commitment to grant levels of authority that match levels of accountability when assigning tasks
- Camaraderie
- The ability to resolve conflicts
- Resiliency
- Managed egos

Review your current organization and team(s). Assign a grade (1 to 5) according to how your organization rates in these areas. Invite others to do the same. Compare your grades and discuss your opinions and options.

INITIAL IMPRESSIONS

HOW DOES THIS SHOW UP FOR ME?

UPON FURTHER REFLECTION

NEXT STEPS

AT THEIR CORE, ORGANIZATIONS ARE NOT ORG CHARTS. THEY ARE TRIBES.

In fact, they are a tribe of tribes. This may initially seem like an odd way to view your organization, but when two or more people come together to accomplish a common goal, tribal dynamics kick in.

Tribes are the most effective model for human collaboration ever established. They are 100 percent responsible for our ability to go from surviving in a harsh, primitive world to dominating and thriving in the modern world. They are in our DNA.

"Birds flock. Fish School. People Tribe."

—Dave Logan, author of Tribal Leadership

Org charts are a tool of the Industrial Age. The emergence of the Innovation Age is rendering them obsolete as the dominant organizational model. Therefore, applying these overly simplistic Newtonian assembly line models to manage groups of intelligent, independent minded, and complex human beings is managerial malpractice in today's knowledge economy.

Viewing your organization through a tribal lens immediately begins to reveal previously hidden human and inter-personal dynamics that drive all performance and profits.

Being unaware of these dynamics makes you vulnerable to them.

16. Practice viewing your organization through a tribal lens compared to an org chart. Notice the promoted behaviors from each model. For instance, how are those in authority viewed? With fear or familiarity? Are people controlled or empowered? Is performance achieved through extrinsic or intrinsic motivations? Etc.

INITIAL IMPRESSIONS

HOW DOES THIS SHOW UP FOR ME?

UPON FURTHER REFLECTION

NEXT STEPS

WE MUST BEWARE OF THE MODELS USED TO DEFINE ORGANIZATIONS BECAUSE THEY DRIVE THE METHODS USED TO ENGAGE THEM.

How we see our organization is how we lead our organization.

Overly linear and hierarchical models produce top-down, command and control leadership thinking, and methods which stifle engagement, productivity, and creativity. All of these reduce profits.

Tribal models inspire communication, cooperation, and collaboration which increase morale performance, innovation, and resiliency. All of these maximize profits.

The goal is to replace rigid structures with adaptive forms that embrace empowerment. The goal is to consider how a new model, one that blends the best of the org chart with the best of the tribe, can be combined to create a much more powerful organization.

Viewing your organization as a tribe coupled with using tribal leadership methods that stress more collaboration, communication, and facilitation will maximize your access to the Bigger Know as well as your ability to monetize it.

Then simply see what you see, and the ideas will come.

17.

INITIAL IMPRESSIONS

HOW DOES THIS SHOW UP FOR ME?

UPON FURTHER REFLECTION

NEXT STEPS

PERHAPS THE MOST IMPORTANT AND VALUABLE DISCOVERY YOU WILL MAKE WHEN VIEWING YOUR ORGANIZATION AS A TRIBE OF TRIBES IS THE EMERGENCE OF "TRIBAL LEADERS" WITHIN THESE "SUB-TRIBES."

Tribal leaders are men and women of great influence who often operate outside of the official leadership structure.

These individuals are empowered by their fellow tribe members because of their wisdom and the loyalty they give to, and therefore receive from, the tribe. This makes them highly influential leaders.

As a result, they are looked to for guidance and council by their peers—especially around issues and initiatives being introduced by management.

The wisest of them are not anti-management because they understand that the tribe's prosperity depends upon healthy collaborations between the front office tribes and the frontline tribes.

Because of their perspective and position, they can be powerful mediators and facilitators.

Look for them. Find them. Engage them. Then watch the possibilities unfurl.

18.

INITIAL IMPRESSIONS

HOW DOES THIS SHOW UP FOR ME?

UPON FURTHER REFLECTION

NEXT STEPS

19.

KNOWLEDGE NETWORKS FOCUS, MOBILIZE, AND LEVERAGE THE BIGGER KNOW OF YOUR ORGANIZATION.

When you think of your teams and departments, think of them as knowledge networks, and when you think of knowledge networks, think of data networks. Both are governed by the same principles because both are information computing and processing networks.

The information processing devices in data networks are computers. In knowledge networks, they are people. You must start with enough of both, and they must have the processing power and capacity to handle expectations.

Computers need specific software and applications to complete their specific tasks. The humans need specific training, knowledge, and experience.

Data networks require high-speed communication links that operate seamlessly to maximize efficiency and effectiveness. Knowledge networks require high degrees of trust, cooperation, and resiliency.

Data networks require access to sufficient bandwidth to handle the expected workload, or they underperform. Human networks require access to sufficient time and resources.

Data networks work best when their managers monitor and support them instead of controlling and interfering with them. Knowledge networks work the same way.

Design, configure, and support your knowledge networks using network principles. If you don't, they will fail. Network principles are unforgiving.

INITIAL IMPRESSIONS

HOW DOES THIS SHOW UP FOR ME?

UPON FURTHER REFLECTION

NEXT STEPS

20.

THE HEALTHIEST, STRONGEST, AND MOST RESILIENT CULTURES ARE THOSE THAT ARE ALLOWED TO FORM BOTH ORGANICALLY AND PURPOSEFULLY.

When attempting to establish a culture, many well-meaning leaders make the mistake of creating it in their own vision or, worse yet, copying another culture.

Cultures are as unique and as complex as the people in them and the environment in which they operate.

High performing cultures are never created by decree from on high. They are created through conversation, collaboration, and alignment between those in the front office and those on the frontline. They are a blend of organic and purposeful design while balancing structure and form.

Front office cultures differ from frontline cultures. Construction cultures differ from academic cultures. For profits differ from nonprofits, corporate differs from small business, and government differs from business. And so it goes and so it should.

The sign of a healthy culture is not in the sameness of rules. It is in the saneness of principles. Are those principles rooted in A.I.R.? If so, allow each group to self-define their acceptable behaviors, traditions, and conventions.

One size will not fit all, but one consciousness can.

CHAPTER TWO

DEVELOPING CONSCIOUS LEADERSHIP SKILLS

IF WE CAN'T LEAD WITH OUR HEARTS, WE CAN'T BE TRUSTED TO LEAD WITH OUR MINDS.

Our hearts are the source of our wisdom, our compassion, our understanding, and our discipline.

When we lead with our hearts, we know when to give council and when to give consequences.

And we care enough to do both.

LEADERS AS ELDERS, STEWARDS, AND TUNING FORKS

INITIAL IMPRESSIONS

HOW DOES THIS SHOW UP FOR ME?

UPON FURTHER REFLECTION

NEXT STEPS

TAKE A MOMENT TO CONSIDER WHAT THE WORD "ELDER" MEANS TO YOU. WHAT FEELINGS AND IMAGES APPEAR? WHAT WORDS COME TO MIND?

Wisdom? Mentor? Honesty? Trusted? Safe? Balanced? Any others?

Think about and reflect upon elders you know or have known. Remember their essence and their impact.

What did they do and how did they do it? What didn't they do and for what reasons? What did they value? What impact have they had, on you and others?

Look for patterns. Search for motives.

What do you admire? What do you aspire to? Where can you begin?

21.

INITIAL IMPRESSIONS

HOW DOES THIS SHOW UP FOR ME?

UPON FURTHER REFLECTION

NEXT STEPS

ELDERS NEITHER APPOINT NOR ANOINT THEMSELVES. THEY DON'T CARE ABOUT ATTENTION OR TITLES. THEY CARE ABOUT THE TRIBE.

They are clear on who they are and what they are here to do. They are not overly affected by either external confirmations or rejections. They know the distractions they create, the ego they activate, and avoid both.

Elders are not in pursuit of leadership roles. They are in pursuit of consciousness. They will only assume leadership roles when and if it becomes clear that doing so will help to further the advancement of the tribe as a whole, and they will step down for the same reason.

They are willing to work to help others, but only those who are willing to work to help themselves. They avoid the trap of enabling weakness.

They are fully committed to, and actively work to develop, train, and support the next generation of conscious leaders. Therefore, you must be committed as well. It is your responsibility and will define your legacy.

Don't make your tribe vulnerable to your absence.

22.

INITIAL IMPRESSIONS

HOW DOES THIS SHOW UP FOR ME?

UPON FURTHER REFLECTION

NEXT STEPS

23.

THE PATH TO SPIRITUAL GROWTH IS ROOTED IN REALITY. IN THE REAL WORLD, IT IS IMPOSSIBLE TO SIT ON A MOUNTAIN TOP AND SIMPLY "ELDER" ALL DAY. NOR CAN WE ALWAYS BE HIGHLY FUNCTIONING BEINGS UNDER ALL CONDITIONS.

We get angry, selfish, jealous, and fearful. That is all part of the human condition and our human consciousness—neither of which will ever go away.

However, we can become more aware of whether it is our human consciousness or our higher consciousness that is driving our thoughts, emotions, and actions.

That awareness allows us to make conscious decisions about whether to succumb to the gravitational pull of our egos or to release that ballast so that we may can rise to a higher level of consciousness.

Therefore, our role as conscious leaders is to courageously seek self-awareness. Seek truth. Then, seek the strength to accept it with grace. But don't do any of it for the purpose of, or in the hopes of, being seen. Do it because you are committed to your growth and are a seeker of wisdom and truth.

Anything else is just the ego parading itself in front of itself for everyone else to see.

INITIAL IMPRESSIONS

HOW DOES THIS SHOW UP FOR ME?

UPON FURTHER REFLECTION

NEXT STEPS

WHEREAS ELDERS ARE THE HOLDERS OF THE WISDOM, THE VISION, AND PRINCIPLES OF THE TRIBE, STEWARDS ARE THOSE WHO ENSURE EACH ARE ACTUALIZED AND IMPLEMENTED. STEWARDS ARE THE CARETAKERS.

While we do not decide if we become an elder of the tribe, that is for others to decide, we can decide to become a steward. Being a steward is a role anyone can assume, and in healthy tribes, many do.

The conscious leader as a steward is like a devoted gardener. They act in service of the garden and relish their role as its caretaker. They know the importance of feeding, weeding, and pruning*— and do all three when needed.

They know whether each plant naturally flowers or bears fruit. How much water does it need? Does it like the sun or wilt from it? Is it high maintenance or low?

They understand how to be responsive to the needs of each plant. Therefore, they understand the importance of treating things equitability as opposed to equally.

How can you mirror the gardener? What do you know about each person? What have you been getting right and what are the benefits? What have you been missing or neglecting and what are the costs?

24.

**Weeding and pruning refers to improving upon or removing any processes, procedures, politics, and even people who inhibit the health, well-being, and production of the tribe.*

INITIAL IMPRESSIONS

HOW DOES THIS SHOW UP FOR ME?

UPON FURTHER REFLECTION

NEXT STEPS

LEADERS WHO ARE STEWARDS ARE LEADERS WHO ARE INFLUENTIAL. THE MORE RESPONSIVE THE LEADER IS TO THE TRIBE, THE MORE RESPONSIVE THE TRIBE WILL BE TO THE LEADER. IT IS UNAVOIDABLE.

Being influential with people yields far superior results than holding power over them. People will always give more when it is their choice. They will always give less when it's demanded from them.

Influence is about giving. Power is about taking. Influence is about trust. Power is about fear. Influence is a result of respecting people. Power is a show of disrespect.

Influence based leaders increase employee engagement which increases profits. Power-based leaders stifle both.

Where are you being power-full and not empowering? When are you showing less respect instead of more? Where are you hurting yourself when you could be helping yourself? What type of culture do you want to create?

Assess and adjust.

25.

INITIAL IMPRESSIONS

HOW DOES THIS SHOW UP FOR ME?

UPON FURTHER REFLECTION

NEXT STEPS

PEOPLE ARE LIKE TUNING FORKS. WE ARE FINELY TUNED, HIGHLY SENSITIZED, AND INTUITIVE SOCIAL CREATURES WHO INSTINCTIVELY PICK UP ON, AND ARE AFFECTED BY, THE ENERGIES OF THOSE AROUND US. THIS DYNAMIC IS A FUNCTION OF PHYSICS THAT AFFECTS BOTH OUR PHYSIOLOGY AND OUR PSYCHOLOGY.

Everything in the universe is, and therefore radiates, energy.

Different levels of consciousness create different energies that vibrate outwardly and affect those around us.

For instance, we have all experienced an angry person or an "Eeyore" entering the room. Even if they don't say anything, we sense their energy and it threatens to shift ours. That shift will occur if we aren't consciously aware of it and either resist it or counter it.

While anyone can affect the energy in a room, leaders tend to do so more because of the amount of influence they are granted or power they exert.

As leaders, our energy sets the tone for the energy of the group. This, in turn, sets the stage for the mood of the group and the consciousness of the group as well.

26. Understand that, as a leader, you are the biggest tuning fork in the group. Be aware, be responsible, and be purposeful with the energy you bring to your interactions.

The energy you put into your world is the energy you create in your world.

✎ INITIAL IMPRESSIONS

✎ HOW DOES THIS SHOW UP FOR ME?

✎ UPON FURTHER REFLECTION

✎ NEXT STEPS

IF WE ARE NOT CONSTANTLY AWARE OF, AND IN CONTROL OF, OUR MOODS AND ENERGIES, WE CREATE CHAOS. THEN WE AND THOSE AROUND US BECOME LIKE TUMBLEWEEDS BEING BLOWN ABOUT BY THE ENERGIES THAT SURROUND US.

When we and/or our teams are under stress, are feeling threatened, or are angry, the emotions and energies can run high. As leaders we must counter this by resonating calm, focused, and productive energies—with integrity.

Conversely, when we and/or our teams are feeling defeated, depressed, or demoralized we must counter that energy by resonating optimistic, determined, and confident energies—with integrity.

This is why it is essential that we regularly practice rising above our emotional energy fields into our more conscious energy fields. Do your best to get present. Get centered. Take a breath. Get perspective and refocus. Wherever you lead yourself is where you will lead your team.

This ability to set the tone is one of the most important traits a conscious leader must develop.

27. Remember this: Before we can lead others to a different consciousness, we must first lead ourselves there. We cannot lead someone to a place we are not.

INITIAL IMPRESSIONS

HOW DOES THIS SHOW UP FOR ME?

UPON FURTHER REFLECTION

NEXT STEPS

AS A LEADER, IT'S IMPORTANT TO KNOW HOW THIS TUNING FORK EFFECT IS CREATED IN ORDER TO PURPOSEFULLY USE IT AND AVOID ACCIDENTALLY MISUSING IT.

Three basic portals vibrate and transmit our energies:

Our words: The words, the tone, the volume, and the speed of our words determine how we are perceived and received. Our energies energize, demoralize, inspire, anger, and even enlighten others. They are powerful communication tools.

Our eyes: We have all experienced the effects a single look can create. Angry, kind, patient, compassionate, condescending, or even disengaged energies are powerfully transmitted by our eyes. It is said that they are the pathways to the soul.

Our bodies: It's scientifically proven by the Heartmath Institute that our bodies generate powerful electromagnetic fields that reach out to others. Those fields are determined by the energies our emotions emit which are driven by the thoughts we embrace.

As a leader, you must be conscious that you are constantly sending messages, knowingly or unknowingly. Therefore, carefully monitor the words you use, the looks you give, and the thoughts you embrace.

28. A good rule of thumb is to always be aware, be purposeful, and be authentic. This is one of the most powerful skills the conscious leader can master.

BLIND SPOTS

It's what we don't know that we don't know that we are most vulnerable to.

Recommended Viewing:

On Being Wrong: Most of us will do anything to avoid being wrong. But what if we're wrong about that? In this TED Talk, "Wrongologist," Kathryn Schulz makes a compelling case for not just admitting but embracing our fallibility. Kathryn Schulz is a staff writer for the New Yorker and is the author of "Being Wrong: Adventures in the Margin of Error."

https://www.ted.com/talks/kathryn_schulz_on_being_wrong

INITIAL IMPRESSIONS

HOW DOES THIS SHOW UP FOR ME?

UPON FURTHER REFLECTION

NEXT STEPS

NEVER UNDERESTIMATE THE IMPORTANCE OF, OR THE VASTNESS OF, WHAT YOU DON'T KNOW.

We know what we know, and we know what we don't know. But we don't know what we don't know that we don't know. For instance, I know that I know how to speak English, and I know that I don't know how to speak Japanese. But what I didn't know was that I had a tendency to be an arrogant leader. That was in my blind spot.

I didn't know that I was, and I didn't know that I didn't know that I was because I couldn't see it, even though everyone else could. Then, because I couldn't see it, I denied it when others tried to show me. All of this made me vulnerable to its effect on me and clueless on its effect on those around me.

It's natural to deny our blind spots and to resist when we're shown them. Their invisibility makes us know that we are right when we couldn't be more wrong, causing us to turn against those who are trying to help us.

The discussion around blind spots often activates egos and emotions which in turn shuts down our openness to their possibility. This is what makes us so vulnerable to them and makes them so dangerous to us.

Discipline yourself to be open to what it is you don't know that you don't know about yourself. Especially when those close to you do.

29.

INITIAL IMPRESSIONS

HOW DOES THIS SHOW UP FOR ME?

UPON FURTHER REFLECTION

NEXT STEPS

BLIND SPOTS ARE LEADERSHIP KILLERS.

They hide the truths that everyone else can see. In fact, they are so well hidden that we often resist seeing, let alone accepting, them even when they're pointed out.

Whether those truths are about our liabilities or our assets, being blind to them limits our abilities to lead because we can't see either the best or worst of our leadership attributes.

Know that you have them.

Be dedicated to finding them.

Be courageous in asking to be shown them.

Be honest with your assessment of them.

Then find the strength to improve upon them. It's always worth it.

INITIAL IMPRESSIONS

HOW DOES THIS SHOW UP FOR ME?

UPON FURTHER REFLECTION

NEXT STEPS

WE CANNOT SEE, THEREFORE WE CANNOT IDENTIFY, OUR OWN BLIND SPOTS. WE NEED HELP IN DOING SO.*

That's why they're called blind spots.

Uncovering blind spots requires help from those who know us well enough to see them and care enough about us to share them.

Pay close attention to those that are most embarrassing or unflattering. But pay even closer attention to those that you initially deny are true.

Those are the sleepers.

Approach them with curiosity about yourself—not criticism towards yourself.

Besides, we all have them. They are a common human trait.

The difference is that the conscious leader seeks to become conscious of them and then becomes committed to addressing them.

**To help uncover your blind spots, experiment with the exercise at the end of this section.*

31.

INITIAL IMPRESSIONS

HOW DOES THIS SHOW UP FOR ME?

UPON FURTHER REFLECTION

NEXT STEPS

NEVER SHOOT THE MESSENGER.

Never make the one you ask for help pay for giving you the help.

That is a betrayal of trust.

Resist the urge to push back, to cut them off, get angry, or be insulted. This will test your commitment to your personal growth in many ways.

Get prepared by centering yourself, and then take nothing personally or as an attack. Instead ask for clarifications. Ask for examples. Ask them to help you see what they see.

Remember to be as open and gracious as possible with those who have agreed to help you. Realize that they are taking a great risk in offering to help you. Make what will be a challenging experience easy on them or you will lose their council.

Their care and respect for you is worthy of your care and respect for them.

Remember: When faced with choosing between truth and ego, choose wisely.

Your ability to lead depends upon it. But your ability to lead a better life depends upon it even more.

32.

INITIAL IMPRESSIONS

HOW DOES THIS SHOW UP FOR ME?

UPON FURTHER REFLECTION

NEXT STEPS

WHEN WE ACT FROM OUR BLIND SPOTS, THOSE AROUND US SEE THEM CLEARLY AND EXPERIENCE THEIR IMPACT. THEN WE EXPERIENCE THEIR IMPACT AS OUR ABILITY TO LEAD ERODES… AND WE WONDER WHY.

The longer the issues in our blind spots go unrecognized, denied, or untreated, the more credibility, influence, and respect we lose.

However, once we acknowledge and address a negative trait, or even a positive one, we had been denying, our credibility and our ability to lead begins to return. People respect those with enough authenticity, integrity, and self-respect to admit weaknesses and improve upon them. We are hardwired to do so.

In doing so, your example will send the message that you stand for creating a culture that values truth and personal growth more than egos. Besides, if you refuse to do your personal work, you will lead many others to refuse to do theirs.

33.

BLIND SPOT EXERCISE

A valuable process to help you identify and begin addressing your blind spots is to identify several people whose feedback you greatly respect, and who you know from different aspects of your life—work, family, friends, volunteers, etc.

Reach out to them with a short, personal questionnaire where you explain that you are on a journey of self-discovery and are seeking to learn things about yourself that may be holding you back by hiding in your blind spots.

Ask them for their honesty and courage to gift you with insights which may help you. You may want to seed their thinking by presenting a few categories where you suspect you may suffer from something hiding in a blind spot.

Be aware of any areas you are resisting knowing about. That is a clue that there is something there. (The ego doesn't like to be busted!)

Also, be careful not to try and control where they go or don't go.

Keep the list to no more than five or six people. This forces you to make the best selections and keeps you from being overwhelmed by too much input.

TIPS

1. Find the courage to do this well. It is not an exercise you will have the chance to repeat anytime soon. (Time is never our friend when identifying issues in our blind spots.)
2. Never make someone pay for telling you the truth. It is a betrayal of their trust.
3. After you get their responses, engage them in a dialogue about what they see. It helps you to get clarification, and it helps them to see that they have not offended you.
4. Think deeply about, and strongly consider, what they offer. Then take what fits and leave what doesn't on the table for future consideration. In time you will either see what they saw, or you will realize that it doesn't apply.
5. Be aware that your ego may try to hijack your higher self's desire to grow. This process will challenge you on levels that may surprise you. It's not for those weak of character.
6. Thank them for their courage to be honest and congratulate yourself for having the courage to seek the truth.

RESPECT YOUR PROCESS

Don't reward progress with punishment.

INITIAL IMPRESSIONS

HOW DOES THIS SHOW UP FOR ME?

UPON FURTHER REFLECTION

NEXT STEPS

34.

WHEN YOUR JOURNEY OF SELF-AWARENESS REVEALS UNCOMFORTABLE FLAWS, DO NOT CRITICIZE OR BERATE YOURSELF. CONGRATULATE YOURSELF.

Just because you may not like an aspect of your past, your present, or your personality doesn't mean that you should not honor and believe in the rest of you.

Acknowledge the errors of your ways. Take responsibility for your actions and make amends if necessary. Then do the work of adjusting your behavior.

Acknowledge yourself for doing the difficult work that is helping you to grow toward your next level. This will help you to have compassion for, and even possibly help, the person next to you who is going through struggles as they are seeking to grow.

INITIAL IMPRESSIONS

HOW DOES THIS SHOW UP FOR ME?

UPON FURTHER REFLECTION

NEXT STEPS

DON'T FOCUS ON THE "BLACK DOT."

We are all a complex mix of dark and light energies and aspects.

Often times, when we uncover a negative trait hiding in a blind spot, it becomes like a black dot on an otherwise white screen. It becomes all that we can see despite the rest being clean.

Beware of the ego's tendency to weaponize an unflattering truth. You may be tempted to chew on it like a dog on a bone. Avoid that trap. It is toxic.

Do not make it too painful to acknowledge, engage, and learn from your weaknesses. Otherwise you will turn what is potentially a blessing of a lesson into a bitter pill which you will refuse to accept.

Don't reward your willingness and courage to grow with violence.

35.

INITIAL IMPRESSIONS

HOW DOES THIS SHOW UP FOR ME?

UPON FURTHER REFLECTION

NEXT STEPS

WHEN WE FOCUS UPON SOMETHING, WE GIVE IT ENERGY AND THAT ENERGY BRINGS IT TO LIFE. WHAT RECEIVES ENERGY AND LIFE GROWS, WHETHER WE WANT IT TO OR NOT.

Therefore, focus on acknowledging and building your positives even while acknowledging and reducing your negatives.

In doing so, you are feeding your positives and pruning your negatives. This accelerates your growth as you simultaneously build your strengths while lessening your weaknesses in that you then begin benefiting from what is known spiritually as the "law of economy."

By engaging the law of economy, you create a cycle of positivity that begins to build upon itself, creating more positivity in areas you never anticipated, as long as you keep the momentum going.

36.

INITIAL IMPRESSIONS

HOW DOES THIS SHOW UP FOR ME?

UPON FURTHER REFLECTION

NEXT STEPS

ONE OF THE MOST IMPORTANT MOTIVATORS IN BEING A CONSCIOUS LEADER IS REMEMBERING WHEN YOU WEREN'T.

When a negative becomes the source of a positive, it ceases to be a negative. When our failures lead to our successes, they are no longer failures. They are lessons.

As you grow in consciousness, you will find that you naturally begin experiencing more inner peace. Your energy shifts. Because of the tuning fork effect, you also radiate a more calm and peaceful energy to those around you which helps to shift their energy.

The law of economy then kicks in. You create less drama for yourself which creates less drama for others. You also become less affected by the drama created by others. You gain more patience, so you have more patience to give others in that you experience less stress for yourself and generate less stress for others.

All of which brings an increased sense of inner peace that you begin to value and work to maintain. This then becomes the motivation to continue building upon this positive cycle and inspires others to do the same.

The law of economy continues to support the work you are doing and the consciousness you are living—consciously use it.

37.

INITIAL IMPRESSIONS

HOW DOES THIS SHOW UP FOR ME?

UPON FURTHER REFLECTION

NEXT STEPS

OBSERVE YOURSELF. LEARN YOURSELF. UNDERSTAND YOURSELF. ACCEPT YOURSELF. RESPECT YOURSELF. LOVE YOURSELF.

Then see yourself in others and see others in yourself.

Jesus said, "Love your neighbor as you love yourself."

Most people think he was just talking about the importance of loving your neighbor. That is not true. His was saying to learn to love and respect ourselves first before trying to love and respect others.

We can't do for others what we haven't first learned to do for ourselves.

Learning to respect ourselves as we grow ourselves can be extremely challenging. But once we do, we are then in a position to understand what it takes to help lead others to do the same.

Helping to lead another through a healthy process of self-discovery and personal growth will be one of the most important things you can do for them and one of the most rewarding things you can do for yourself.

But first, you must learn to be patient and kind with yourself, as well as respectful and tolerant and encouraging and forgiving.

We can't do for others what we haven't first learned to do for ourselves.

38.

INITIAL IMPRESSIONS

HOW DOES THIS SHOW UP FOR ME?

UPON FURTHER REFLECTION

NEXT STEPS

THE FOLLOWING IS A PRAYER OF SELF-ACCEPTANCE, SELF-RESPECT, AND A COMMITMENT TO PERSONAL GROWTH. IT HAS SERVED ME EXTREMELY WELL DURING SOME OF MY MOST CHALLENGING TIMES OF SELF-DISCOVERY AND SELF-REALIZATION.

"I am who I am because this one is like that.
And I will be that with as much grace as I can muster."

I don't need to justify or explain who I am. I just need to be authentic with myself and to others.

I don't need permission or approval to be who I am. I just need to be gracious and respectful towards others.

I don't even have to understand why I am the way I am. I just need to understand that I am a work in progress working to make more progress.

Then I must embrace the fact that you are too.

39.

BEWARE OF PITFALLS

Vanity, Anger, Being Critical,
Gossip, Loneliness

Watch what you put in play because
the law of cause and effect doesn't play.

"What ye reap so shall ye sow."

"What goes around comes around."

"Karma is a bitch."

INITIAL IMPRESSIONS

HOW DOES THIS SHOW UP FOR ME?

UPON FURTHER REFLECTION

NEXT STEPS

PERHAPS THE WORST PITFALL OF LEADERSHIP IS VANITY. ANY SMALL SUCCESS IN LEADERSHIP COULD BRING VANITY WHICH CAN EASILY SPREAD LIKE A BRUSH FIRE THAT ULTIMATELY BURNS US.

Vanity is our ego in action. It is inflated self-importance that then leads to the expectation of others to recognize this importance and make us a greater person than we really are. This only serves to overfeed our "dog" which causes it to grow larger and become more dominant than is in the best interest of anyone, especially ourselves.

This self-absorbed aspect of our personality is perhaps the greatest threat to our becoming a conscious leader. We must constantly be aware of its lies and its lure. It is a siren on the rocks.

While vanity can deter us, if we domesticate and train it, it can also spur us to reach greater heights. But first we have to learn to be on the lookout for it, monitor it closely, and keep it from becoming over-inflated and counter-productive.

Our vanity excels at consistently hiding in our blind spots!

40.

INITIAL IMPRESSIONS

HOW DOES THIS SHOW UP FOR ME?

UPON FURTHER REFLECTION

NEXT STEPS

41.

VANITY HAS A THOUSAND CLAWS BY WHICH IT CLAIMS ITS VICTIMS. IT IS ONE OF THE MOST HIDDEN ELEMENTS THAT AFFECT OUR CONSCIOUSNESS. IT SHOWS ITSELF IN THE LITTLE THINGS WE DO AND THE WORDS WE SPEAK.

Others recognize it in us before we do. They might even speak to us of it, but we resist recognizing it because our ego is too vain to see its vanity. Such is the dangerously absurd nature of ego. It loves looking into the mirror but can never see anything except our good side, whether it is real or imagined.

To minimize the damage that vanity creates, we must first accept that we all are affected by it. We must then be careful not to demonize it. Instead, be aware of when it is in play, be conscious of how it is challenging us, and then make conscious decisions to not allow it to negatively impact ourselves or others.

Otherwise, we will surely pay the consequences of both a loss of respect and the overall effectiveness that it will always extract.

INITIAL IMPRESSIONS

HOW DOES THIS SHOW UP FOR ME?

UPON FURTHER REFLECTION

NEXT STEPS

BEWARE—AND BE AWARE—OF ANGER. IT IS ALWAYS A TRAP. LEFT UNCHECKED, ANGER BECOMES AN ENORMOUS LIABILITY TO YOUR ABILITY TO LEAD BECAUSE, AT BEST, IT ALIENATES PEOPLE AND, AT WORST, IT MAKES THEM ANGRY.

Whether they experience fear of us, or anger toward us, anger always creates a separation between people that can often last long after the incident itself.

Think of it this way: If you knew someone's dog tended to be mean and had bitten you, or others, would you trust it?

Would you want to engage it, or would you keep your distance from it? Wouldn't you also warn others that his or her dog was mean? Of course you would.

Such is the impact of when you let your "dog" off the leash too easily or too often.

As a leader, undisciplined expressions of anger will cost you more respect, credibility, and influence than even vanity. It is proof of one's immaturity and lack of control. And people don't follow people who lack maturity or self-control.

Learn your triggers. Be conscious of your anger when it appears. Then develop anger release methods that work for you.

42.

Take a walk. Take a moment. Take a breath. Take responsibility.

INITIAL IMPRESSIONS

HOW DOES THIS SHOW UP FOR ME?

UPON FURTHER REFLECTION

NEXT STEPS

THE ANGRIER WE GET, THE DUMBER WE GET.

This is not to say that we should never get angry. Anger has its use and its place. However, it is how we respond to, and use, our anger that either diminishes or adds to our position as leaders.

People process information primarily one of two ways: emotionally or intellectually. To the degree we are doing one, we are not doing the other. They are the oil and water of the human consciousness.

This is not to say that intellect is always good, and emotion is always bad. That would be absurd as each plays an important role in our ability to live a healthy life. However, it is up to us to learn how to achieve the right balance or we will experience the consequences.

Anger issues hide extremely well in our blind spots. Almost everyone who has anger issues has no clue they do. They are convinced that most of their anger is due to other people when the truth is that we are always responsible for our own anger.

This doesn't mean we should never get angry. Anger, like vanity, plays a valuable role in our lives, as long as it released appropriately.

Aristotle provided excellent guidelines for leaders dealing with anger when he said:

> *"Anyone can become angry—that is easy. But to be angry with the right person, to the right degree, at the right time, for the right purpose, and in the right way—that is not within everybody's power and is not easy."*

43.

Try to do your best in this space. And when you get it wrong, make amends, make apologies, and make adjustments to your behavior.

INITIAL IMPRESSIONS

HOW DOES THIS SHOW UP FOR ME?

UPON FURTHER REFLECTION

NEXT STEPS

BEING HIGHLY CRITICAL TOWARDS OTHERS ALWAYS COSTS US AS LEADERS.

As leaders, we are judged based upon how we judge, treat, and speak of others.

While we cannot prevent ourselves from thinking critical thoughts, we must resist the temptation to allow them to control our actions because they will ultimately define our entire culture.

Therefore, become aware of when you are feeling the urge to be critical of others. Recognize your triggers. Then, be alert to how your words, eyes, and body language may be transmitting any critical thoughts you are having but do not intend to be sending.

Being critical is also a sign of arrogance. Arrogance repels people which then significantly impairs your ability to lead. Arrogance also hides in our blind spots.

In fact, I was blind to my tendencies to be arrogant until, much to my surprise, I was shown how often it came out. At first, I was too blind to see it. Then I was too vain to admit it—until I simply couldn't deny it.

Our weaknesses often work in concert to hide one another. Vanity hides our arrogance. Arrogance hides our insecurities. And it is our insecurities that cause us to be criticizers instead of coaches.

INITIAL IMPRESSIONS

HOW DOES THIS SHOW UP FOR ME?

UPON FURTHER REFLECTION

NEXT STEPS

BEING CRITICAL OF ANOTHER INSTEAD OF BEING CONSTRUCTIVE COMBINES THREE OTHER MAJOR PITFALLS OF LEADERSHIP: VANITY, ANGER, AND ARROGANCE.

Therefore, as conscious leaders, we must be eternally vigilant to ensure the avoidance of criticism and instead focus upon coaching.

People instinctively know when someone is criticizing them instead of coaching them and they don't like it. So, a counterproductive and adversarial relationship is created.

Therefore, as a conscious leader, our goal is to always coach not to criticize.

While it is natural to feel frustrated and even angry toward others, we must resist the impulse to act on the urges of our egos and emotions. But we cannot simply stop one behavior without replacing it with another. So, replace the urge to criticize with a commitment to coach. And remember:

- Criticism is all about you. Coaching is all about them.
- Criticism is an egotistical reaction. Coaching is a thoughtful response.
- Criticism weakens relationships. Coaching strengthens them.
- Criticism creates retaliation. Coaching increases collaboration.
- Criticism restricts learning. Coaching advances it.

45. Conscious leaders coach.

**Principle 6 of the Bigger Know Principles of leadership*

INITIAL IMPRESSIONS

HOW DOES THIS SHOW UP FOR ME?

UPON FURTHER REFLECTION

NEXT STEPS

GOSSIP IS INSIDIOUS.

Leaders who engage in gossip have fallen prey to many of the pitfalls that must be avoided: vanity, anger, arrogance, and their insecurities.

When a leader becomes a gossip, they destroy their ability to lead because gossipers are never respected. Gossip always pits people against one another; therefore, it always weakens the tribe. True leaders never seek to weaken others or the tribe.

Gossip is also dangerous to the culture because of its tendency to go viral. Science has proven when people gossip it releases endorphins that make them feel a sense of elation. It also gives them a sense of superiority. So chronic gossipers gossip to get their fix. They love the endorphins that the feeling of being superior and being the center of attention releases for them. So, they tend to repeat the same stories and are always on the lookout for new stories about new people to inject into the tribe. The drug of gossip can become highly addictive.

As a leader, you must be careful to never gossip and be on high alert for habitual gossipers. They must be dealt with.

While we can never expect to create a gossip-free environment, we must be diligent to limit it and work to make it culturally frowned upon.

Gossip is not a victimless crime.

46.

INITIAL IMPRESSIONS

HOW DOES THIS SHOW UP FOR ME?

UPON FURTHER REFLECTION

NEXT STEPS

GOSSIPING FEELS DANGEROUSLY SATISFYING BECAUSE IT FEEDS THE EGO. EGOS LIKE TO BE FED. WHAT WE FEED GROWS. EGOS LIKE TO GROW.

As conscious leaders, we must avoid gossip like the drug it is, and we must work to keep it from infiltrating our tribes. No one is immune to its lure. It is part of the human consciousness.

If and when you catch yourself engaging in it, acknowledge it and stop it. Be the example. If and when you catch others engaging in it, clearly address it, but do so diplomatically. Then be sure to set the example with your own actions.

Gossip is tantalizingly easy to fall into. But most people are embarrassed when they either realize they are engaging in it or are caught doing it. So most of the time it is not essential to make a big deal out of it when you encounter it. It is, however, essential that you send the message that it's not acceptable.

Be careful to remember that a leader who engages in gossip does far more damage to themselves than to their target. And that damage is imperceptible until it's too late.

47.

INITIAL IMPRESSIONS

HOW DOES THIS SHOW UP FOR ME?

UPON FURTHER REFLECTION

NEXT STEPS

48.

LEADERSHIP OFTEN LEADS TO A SENSE OF LONELINESS.

Leadership is highly rewarding, however, expect to experience a sense of loneliness. Loneliness is dangerous to your standing as a leader because, if unchecked, loneliness leads to self-pity which leads to self-absorption and a feeling of being victimized. And victimization almost always leads to some form of retaliation. It also stands to reason that one can't be both a victim and a leader.

Expect to be misunderstood. Expect to make hard decisions without showing your emotions. Expect to hurt and to have others think you're cold. Expect to be unable to share all you know or to explain all your reasons. Expect to make many big decisions alone. Expect to have some people leave when it gets tough because they can. Expect to do the hardest tasks. Expect the pressure.

Then relish in it all. Use it to refine you, redefine you, teach you, and grow you. Turn everything into a lesson. You are paying one hell of a tuition, so ace the class.

When you're feeling alone ask yourself: "What am I being taught?" not: "Why is this happening to me?" Asking yourself what you are being taught is a far more powerful and productive question. It's the difference between being a leader or being a victim.

That was the question I asked when I was diagnosed with stage four cancer and it transformed everything.

Expect it all. Embrace it all. Endure it all. And then do it all without losing your compassion or humanity. It will grow you as a leader. That is its purpose.

Then find other leaders who understand so you're not as lonely.

CHAPTER 3

DEVELOPING RESILIENT CULTURES

"Culture eats strategy for breakfast."

—Peter Drucker

RESILIENCY IS SUPERIOR TO SUSTAINABILITY.

Resiliency is superior to sustainability.

Sustainability is the ability to maintain status quo under stresses and over time.

Resiliency is the ability to become stronger under stresses and over time.

As leaders we must create the conditions that turn adversities into advantages and teach others to do the same.

Doing so will makes us all stronger, wiser, and ultimately safer.

That is the power of resiliency.

INITIAL IMPRESSIONS

HOW DOES THIS SHOW UP FOR ME?

UPON FURTHER REFLECTION

NEXT STEPS

TO CREATE RESILIENT CULTURES WE MUST CREATE CONDITIONS UNDER WHICH THEY WILL FORM.

The tools that create cultural conditions are called laws. The moral quality of a culture's laws coupled with the consistency of their enforcement defines the consciousness of a culture.

There are two types of laws: common and political. Common law is rooted in moral, ethical, and religious thought. Political law has no such foundation. They're created by those in power. If they change their minds, they change the laws.

Richard Maybury, after years of research of many religious and philosophical teachings, has identified two laws that are at the foundation of all common law. They are:

"(1) Do all you have agreed to do, and (2) do not encroach on other persons or their property."

The first of Maybury's laws speaks to acting with uncompromising integrity. It also requires that any agreements are made with free will and without coercion or threat from others. It is the basis for all contract law.

Maybury's second law protects an individual's rights and possessions. It's the basis for all criminal and tort law. These laws, while only seventeen words, must be interpreted literally and precisely to be effective.

49. Common law uses moral principles to protect the powerless. Political law uses power and force to exploit the powerless. Common law creates resilient cultures Political law kills them.

INITIAL IMPRESSIONS

HOW DOES THIS SHOW UP FOR ME?

UPON FURTHER REFLECTION

NEXT STEPS

THERE ARE MANY TYPES OF HEALTHY CULTURES AND MANY WAYS TO GROW THEM.

When working on your culture, resist the urge to either create a one-size-fits-all structure or strictly mimic another company's culture. It simply won't work because: "They ain't you and you ain't them."

The most resilient cultures respect and reflect the uniqueness of the individuals in them, including the leaders, but not exclusive to them.

As a leader, don't act as an engineer who tries to build a culture using a strict formula. Instead, act as a gardener who creates the conditions that allow the most natural and healthiest culture to emerge from the people.

You can begin this by having purposeful conversations with the people involved. Ask for their opinions, suggestions, and insights. Be genuinely curious about, and open to, their input. Empower them in the conversation.

Be open to the possibility that the culture may already be healthy and that not much change is needed. But, it may be also be sick, and that sickness may be coming from management. Be open to hearing the truth and create a safe environment for it to be told.

If they feel it is sick, it is essential that you challenge yourself to not be defensive, dismissive, or controlling. Take nothing personally and make no one pay for their honesty.

50.

If you do this well, it will not only increase the health of your culture, it will also significantly increase your standing as a leader within it.

THE IMPORTANCE OF CONFLICTS AND CONSEQUENCES

Conflict and consequences are essential components to building a resilient culture.

When properly acknowledged and addressed, both become productive catalysts for individual and institutional growth.

When avoided or ignored, both become hydras that spawn even more conflict and consequences.

INITIAL IMPRESSIONS

HOW DOES THIS SHOW UP FOR ME?

UPON FURTHER REFLECTION

NEXT STEPS

CONFLICTS ARE NOT BAD. THEY ARE NATURAL. THEY SHOULD NOT BE AVOIDED. THEY SHOULD BE EXPLORED.

As long as there are people, there will be conflicts. Conflicts are not problems unless emotions turn them into confrontations.

Conscious leaders turn conflicts into conversations that address issues before they become emotional and confrontational. They work to culturally rebrand conflicts into early warning signs that something important needs to be addressed.

Discuss with your team the need to make this shift in perspective. Empower them and expect them to develop processes they can use to diffuse situations before they escalate. Encourage them to use less fight or flight emotion and more openness and intellectual curiosity.

Make yourself available as a mediator but not as their first option. Then if asked to resolve a situation become emotionally neutral before getting involved. You can't lead them away from emotions if you are embroiled in them yourself.

Begin by sincerely listening to each person's side. Clearly understand each person's point of view. Do not outwardly take a side but, after listening and assessing, help them find their compromise. Be the calming presence. Use your tuning fork.

51. The more effective you become at turning conflicts into conversations the more effective you become at turning adversity into assets.

✎ INITIAL IMPRESSIONS

✎ HOW DOES THIS SHOW UP FOR ME?

✎ UPON FURTHER REFLECTION

✎ NEXT STEPS

A CULTURE WITHOUT CONSEQUENCES IS A CULTURE IN CHAOS.

CONSEQUENCES: *NOUN – A result or effect of an action or condition.*

Healthy consequences are not negative, nor are they a punishment. They are teachers.

Dan Millman states, "The universe does not judge us; it only provides consequences and lessons and opportunities to balance and learn through the law of cause and effect."

All cultures have laws and they have consequences designed to maintain those laws. Violations are often tiered and can be categorized as misdemeanors, felonies, and capital offenses, each having consequences commensurate with the level of offense(s) committed.

When trying to identify which offenses should receive what level of consequences, it may be helpful to think of misdemeanors as "C'mon man!" offenses that get verbal warnings; felonies as "three strikes and you're out" offenses that get written warnings; and capital offenses as "one and done" offenses that result in immediate termination.

As a leader, it is imperative you ensure the above details are not only clearly defined and understood but also fairly and consistently administered. Failure to be consistent with company consequences could result in your experiencing legal consequences by mistreated employees.

52. This a very challenging aspect of conscious leadership and will test you often. Get it wrong and the consequences will be painful. Get it right and the consequences will be rewarding.

Either way you will learn something because consequences are our teachers.

WIT AND WISDOM

53.

IF YOU TREAT THEM LIKE PRISONERS EXPECT A JAIL BREAK. IF YOU THINK THEY ARE FOOLS YOU WILL BE OUTSMARTED. REMEMBER: NO ONE IS POWERLESS. JUST ASK MARIE ANTOINETTE.

54.

"NEVER TRY TO TEACH A PIG TO SING. IT IS FRUSTRATING FOR YOU. AND IT IRRITATES THE PIG." —ANONYMOUS

Just because you want, or need, someone to be good at something does not mean they could be, should be, or—more importantly—want to be.

Not everyone has the capability or the desire you want them to have to do the job you want them to do. As much as possible, pay attention to their unique abilities and strengths and avoid their weaknesses and resistances.

If the disparity between what you need them to do and what they can do or are willing to do is too great, then accept that reality and make a change.

BEWARE OF HIGH MAINTENANCE LOW PERFORMERS. THEY GENERATE A LOT OF STRESS AND AGGRAVATION WHILE PROVIDING LITTLE VALUE.

When confronted, they will try to convince you that you, or other people or circumstances, are the source of the problems they are causing. They will show an unwillingness to take responsibility or steps to improve.

You can often recognize these types of people because they speak fluent "victimese."

Sometimes they truly believe what they say. Other times they are purposefully being manipulative and passive aggressive.

Either way, only help them to see the error of their ways if they are willing to take responsibility for their actions. If they aren't, do not take their bait and don't take on their problems.

Be prepared for this to be a terminal condition for which the only cure may be termination.

55.

56.

IF YOU ENABLE SNOWFLAKES, DON'T BE SURPRISED WHEN YOU GET HIT WITH AN AVALANCHE OF WEAKNESS, WHINING, AND ENTITLEMENTS.

There is real value in being rough and edgy when that's the right tool for the job.

57.

"THE NEXT TIME YOU THINK YOU ARE SOMEONE OF GREAT IMPORTANCE TRY ORDERING ANOTHER MAN'S DOG AROUND."
—ANONYMOUS

58.

BEING FRUSTRATED THAT PEOPLE DON'T THINK LIKE YOU IS LIKE BEING FRUSTRATED THAT THEY DON'T LOOK LIKE YOU.

They don't because they don't.

Instead, focus upon understanding how and why they think the way they think. Either their thinking may change your thinking, or you will understand how to help to change theirs.

Along the way, be mindful that a different way is not always a wrong way. Oftentimes, there are many ways to think about the same thing without any of them being wrong.

59.

CONTROL IS THE DARK SIDE OF HELP.

60.

RESIST THE URGE TO ALWAYS HAVE QUICK ANSWERS. HAVE THE PATIENCE TO ALLOW FOR EVENTS TO UNFOLD ENOUGH TO UNDERSTAND THE DYNAMICS THAT ARE IN PLAY. BUT BE CAREFUL. PROCRASTINATION MASKS ITSELF AS PATIENCE TO THE TIMID OR LAZY.

61.

AS A LEADER, YOUR FIRST ROLE IS TO OBSERVE—THEN TO ASSESS—THEN TO ACT. ONLY THE FOOLISH AND INEXPERIENCED REVERSE THIS ORDER.

BEWARE THAT WHAT YOU WEAPONIZE WILL EVENTUALLY BE USED AGAINST YOU. WHETHER IT BE WORDS, POWER, DISRESPECT, OR EVEN HUMOR.

62.

"ARGUING WITH SOME PEOPLE IS LIKE WRESTLING WITH A PIG IN THE MUD. SOONER OR LATER YOU REALIZE THAT THE PIG LIKES THE MUD." —ANONYMOUS

63.

DO NOT CONFUSE A HIGH DEGREE OF INTELLIGENCE WITH A HIGH DEGREE OF CONSCIOUSNESS. HISTORY IS FILLED WITH HIGHLY INTELLIGENT PEOPLE WHO POSSESSED EXCEPTIONALLY LOW LEVELS OF CONSCIOUSNESS.

64.

KNOW WHEN TO REST AND BE STRONG ENOUGH TO DO SO.

65.

66.

NEVER APOLOGIZE IF YOU DON'T MEAN IT. PEOPLE WILL SENSE THE INSINCERITY AND WILL RESENT YOU FOR IT. PLUS, TO APOLOGIZE FOR SOMETHING YOU AREN'T SORRY FOR IS A LIE. DON'T LIE.

67.

MINDSET IS EVERYTHING. YOURS FIRST. THEIRS SECOND.

RESISTANCE IS OFTEN THE CHILD OF FRUSTRATION. FRUSTRATION IS THE CHILD OF CONFUSION. COMMUNICATION IS THE ANTIDOTE TO BOTH. COMMUNICATION IS THE LUBRICATION THAT KEEPS THE ORGANIZATION RUNNING SMOOTHLY.

68.

NO ONE CAN EVER MAKE YOU GIVE UP. THAT IS ALWAYS A PERSONAL DECISION THAT NO ONE CAN EVER TAKE FROM YOU.

Deciding to no longer do something that is not working for you is not quitting. It's about being wise enough, independent enough, and determined enough to keep searching to find what is waiting for you.

69.

70.

ONE OF THE MOST VALUABLE THINGS YOU CAN GIVE THE PEOPLE YOU ARE LEADING IS CREDIT.

It validates them, it rewards them, it empowers them, and it encourages them. All of this increases employee engagement.

71.

RECOGNIZE YOUR TRIGGERS AND BE ON THE LOOKOUT FOR WHAT TRIGGERS OTHERS. IT HELPS AVOID UNPRODUCTIVE AND VOLATILE REACTIONS.

72.

FIVE QUESTIONS YOU CAN ASK WHEN WORKING WITH SOMEONE WHO IS ENGAGING IN COUNTERPRODUCTIVE BEHAVIORS ARE:

1. How is that working for you?
2. What is, or was, your part in the situation?
3. What might you do, or could have done, differently that could create a more favorable result?
4. Have you had enough yet?
5. What can I do to support you in changing your behavior?

73.

THE MINUTE I MAKE LEADERSHIP ABOUT ME I HAVE STOPPED LEADING THEM AND STARTED PUSHING THEM.

74. MAINTAIN PERSPECTIVE. WHEN YOU'RE FEELING YOURSELF BEING PUZZLED BY CIRCUMSTANCES, TAKE THE POSITION OF THE OBSERVER.

Imagine yourself in a hot air balloon rising above the situation. Take a breath and take a 360-degree look around you. From this higher perspective you will be able to see the landscape more clearly.

This will also allow you to rise above your confusion to access ideas, insights, and your intuition. And as you do, remember to ask yourself: What class am I in and why?

---

75. CONSCIOUS LEADERS CREATE A SENSE OF BELONGING. IN DOING SO THEY SATISFY ONE OF OUR MOST BASIC NEEDS—TO BE A WELCOME PART OF A TRIBE.

Without a sense of belonging, people become self-centered and refuse to sacrifice for the tribe. And why should they? If they don't feel valued and protected by the tribe, why would they value or protect the tribe? What goes around comes around. What we give we get.

IT'S NOT ABOUT EQUALITY. IT IS ABOUT EQUITY. NOT EVERY PLANT NEEDS THE SAME AMOUNT OF SUNLIGHT OR WATER TO FLOURISH. WHAT CAUSES ONE PERSON TO THRIVE MAY CAUSE THE OTHER TO WITHER. BE A WISE AND RESPONSIVE GARDENER.

76.

GREAT LEADERS KNOW THAT CREATING THE CONDITIONS FOR SUCCESS IS THE MOST IMPORTANT STEP THAT LEADS TO SUCCESS.

77.

ADDITIONAL RESOURCES

Recommended Reading

Each of these books has significantly helped shape my development.

The Road to Spiritual Freedom - Harold Kemp

Whatever Happened to Justice - Richard Maybury

The Tao of Leadership - John Heider

Tribal Leadership - Dave Logan, John King, and Hale Fisher-Wright

Leaders Eat Last - Simon Sinek

The True Believer - Eric Hoffer

Black Elk - The Sacred Ways of a Lakota - Wallace Black Elk and William S. Lyon

Just Listen - Mark Goulston

Leadership and Self-Deception - The Arbinger Institute

The Elder - Dr. Marc B. Cooper and James C. Selman

Seven Principles for Living with Authenticity - Jack Beauregard

Wolves Change Rivers - Dan Guglielmo

Guide to a Richer Life: Know Your Worth, Find Your Voice, Speak Your Mind - Donna Rustigian Mac

Recommended Videos

HUMAN Extended version VOL.1 by Yann Arthus-Bertrand: To view this is to connect with humanity in a most powerful way. Arthus-Bertrand asks why, from one generation to the next, do we continue to make the same mistakes? What does it mean to be a human today? Do we not all have the same values? This video and the others in the series allow everyone to see the human in the human in us all.

https://www.youtube.com/watch?v=vdb4XGVTHkE

Stand by Me / Playing for Change: We are all the same. We all seek love. We all need support. We all long to be seen and to be heard. And we all crave a true sense of belonging. People are people. Music is music. And soul equals soul.

https://www.youtube.com/watch?v=Us-TVg40ExM

ABOUT THE AUTHOR

Jeffrey Deckman is an award-winning serial entrepreneur who has spent over thirty-five years founding and building companies—two of which became multimillion-dollar firms in the technology sectors. In 2005 he founded Capability Accelerators as a way to help business owners and executives take their organizations and leadership teams to the next level using twenty-first century processes.

His entire career has been spent in the trenches and has spanned from the front lines to the front office as he rose from being a lineman and tower worker to the CEO of his telecommunications integration firm. He has built nonprofits, political organizations, and was a founding partner in a twenty-first century think tank. He has also been appointed by three Rhode Island governors to serve on economic development and workforce development initiatives.

Jeffrey is a stage 4 cancer survivor who has been a dedicated student of the Eckankar and Taoist teachings for decades, including having studied extensively under a shaman for twelve years. He is a Level II Reiki practitioner, a certified practitioner of restorative justice, and a student of Quantum-Touch energy healing.

He is an innovative thought leader in the development of the new conscious leadership and organizational design models in demand by the modern worker in the modern workplace in the modern knowledge economy.

Contact Jeffrey at:

https://www.jeffreydeckman.com

Jeffrey@JeffreyDeckman.com

Made in the USA
Middletown, DE
09 April 2019